W9-BIX-991

How Formal?

poems by

Stephanie Barbé Hammer

block prints by

Ann Brantingham

Spout Hill Press

First Edition

April 2014

Copyright ©2014 by Stephanie Barbé Hammer

All rights reserved.

For information about permission to reproduce selections from this book, contact Spout Hill Press at spouthillpress@aol.com.

www.spouthillpress.com

Seal Beach, California

Cover design by Ann Brantingham

ISBN 13: 978-0615988412

ISBN 10: 0615988415

How Formal?

poems by

Stephanie Barbé Hammer

Also by Stephanie Barbé Hammer

Sex with Buildings (2012)

Schiller's Wound: The Theater of Trauma from Crisis to Commodity (2001)

The Sublime Crime: Fascination, Failure, and Form in Literature of the Enlightenment (1994)

For My Family

Foreword

Rarely in the poetry world does a new voice emerge in such a complete and well-developed debut as does Stephanie Hammer's in this volume. In fact, it feels nearly deceptive to call *How Formal?* a debut collection, for Hammer is a poet who brings a lifetime's worth of lyrical moves to the page; she floats effortlessly through styles, forms, tones, and ranges of surprising content—all with a mature, lively voice toward which most poets can only strive.

To enter into the poems before you is to plant a foot on what seems to be familiar terrain, only to feel the ground slope away or to rise to hold you at the most unexpected of places. The organizational premise of *How Formal?*, for example, seems straightforward enough: a literary tour of the received forms, invented forms, free verse, experimental styles, and palimpsests. Yet Hammer succeeds in upsetting our expectations of what her poems might do. If we're lulled into assuming that sestina or ottava rima, by virtue of their formality, will be buttoned-up, or if we suppose that her free verses will trace the traditional territory of the personal or confessional, the ground that we've supposed to be flat begins to undulate beneath us, and gives us unexpected textures and surprising nuances to explore. These poems subvert our expectation with formal and semi-formal work that looks candidly, boldly, and even plain-spokenly at that which is most personal, as in "Ottava non-rima per noi (for us)":

> *"...I want all our love unvarnished,*
> *Uncontained, unrepentant. I want to sit with you at this*
> > *stupid fucking table and*
> *Remember your grandmother and even my terrifying former*
> > *girlfriend's terrifying*
> *Mater, and all our crazy bitch relations."*

So too does Hammer give us freer styles that deal with the most public of issues and our collective wounds as a modern world:

> There are too many skulls. The Koreans say so, and the
> > Germans say so, and the
> Sudanese say so, and some Israelis and some Palestinians—
> > mostly women—say so too...
> I'll tell you what else say the women in black, I'll tell you what
> > else say the widows in
> Ozxaca, in Belfast, in Brooklyn, in Bangladesh, in Homs.
> > There is something else.
>
> > > --"Skulls"

In this depth and expanse of what concerns Hammer in *How Formal?*, what becomes abundantly clear as the collection progresses is that Hammer could run intellectual circles around most readers if she wished. Her poems seamlessly integrate literary theory, Midrash, languages from Hebrew to French, the Classics, and much greater than a mere working knowledge of writers from Camus to Rushdie—all in musical, rhythmically satisfying verse. But while such a richness of knowledge and range of reference could easily skew toward the showy or the erudite for erudition's sake, Hammer's poems illuminate rather than obfuscate. In part, she achieves this accessible aesthetic by using a liberal dose of delightful, whimsical surprises. Indeed, *How Formal?* sings with the gleefully irreverent, as with Devorah peeking out from the Torah to tell us that she sits beneath a tree not to avoid offending the community's prickly men but because it's appallingly hot in Judea. Equally witty is a poem in which a child defenestrates a rubber prince action-figure from a high-rise apartment with an exuberant *"away with ye."* In a lesser writer's work, such vivid, off-beat romps might be the beginning and end of the poems' projects. But in Hammer's work, the derisive is never gratuitous; a tremendous and even painful honesty glows beneath the humor in the collection. Hammer is a poet who is unafraid to look fully at what cuts most deeply beneath the absurd:

> I convert. My mother is furious. I feel cheated, she said. My
> father is dead and she's an atheist. You're with THEM now,
> she says...According to orthodox Rabbis I'm not really
> Jewish. I find this oddly comforting. If another Holocaust
> comes, I can go to the gas, feeling slightly superior, knowing I
> have chosen the showers, not had them chosen for me.

> --"Ars Judaica"

Perhaps the unifying principle of the poems you hold in your hands is not so much the evolving formats of pieces from the strict to the experimental, but the walk Hammer takes the reader on through the private, the public, and finally through the intersections between two spaces. Along that walk, with its terrain both challenging and smooth at intervals, both delightful and unsettling as it unfolds, each footfall leads us into the unknown and yet, somehow, closer to home.

Kelly Davio
February 12, 2014
Los Angeles

Table of Contents

Formless

Transformative (translations, adaptations, palimpsests)

Formal

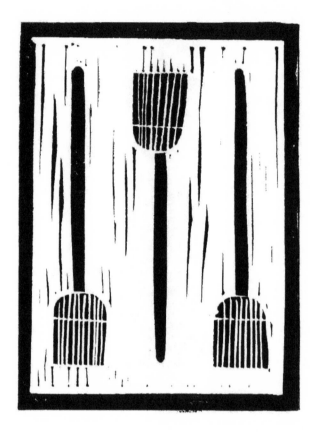

Sestina – Macbethian

Beware, Mom said: the young imagine bicycles ridden by wicked
witches who shall fall under the hurtling houses. None
shall speak their names, she said they said. But hush —— Even if you turn
out to be an old woman, she whispered, don't tell the myth you know –
Or say that you know anything. It's not safe to be older, and even if they listen
to you, that's when you're in mucho trouble double.

I glimpse the dangerous truth: I see the women who are not double
my age. They're 10 years older max, looking desperate and confused; not wicked
old ladies. Not even. Just smart startled women whose surprised eyes say *listen*
to me won't you please? Today was like that. A woman with a nun's
frantic blue-eyed gaze leapt at me at a bookstore reading, said "Do you know
the author?" I said "Slightly. He's my colleague. You?" She turned

away looked wildly for something, eyes rotating back. "Yes," she said. "We took
                turns
waiting for a taxi at JFK airport. It's how we met. We doubled
up. Shared a limo. Taxis are impossible to find there, so we said No
to the yellow cab people. They are such monsters. Really wicked."
"That's how it is in New York" I said. "People are just, well, mean." "Nonsense"
She said. "There's no excuse for meanness. Are you listening?"

"Yes," I tried to reassure her. "I am paying attention as hard as I can, I will listen
to you, as long as you need me to." So -- she kept talking, her lips turned
cartwheels she had too much to say and no time to say it. None.
I took a deep breath as another woman slightly younger did a double
take at our conversation. "Can I join in?" she said. "I am not wicked
And I am so alone. No one knows me. No one listens and I don't even know

myself if I matter or even if I'm alive. Do you ever feel like that?" "No"
I answered but I was lying. I feel like that always, like no one is listening
Like no one cares except the scary man on the metro who said I was wicked
as he grabbed my leg. "I know you," he said, "I know who you are. Don't you turn
away from me – bitch." But I slipped past him and out the sliding doors. Know
this: the only people who see me are mashers on trains or none.

Not even these weird sisters. Now I sit between the younger woman and the nun
lady who once limoed with the author. They ask do I happen to know
the best health care plan for women. I say "Blue Cross." They sob. I've got double

dames on my hands, and now they discuss the poisonous environment. I listen
to a description of sulfuric acid in creeks. The talk moves to cell towers. I turn
hoping the author will finally start reading. And guess what? He reads of wicked

witches. My neighbors listen intently. I don't. I can't. The nun
lady sighs. The other woman still weeps. I turn again, look for the exit. I know
they balance on bikes of perceived wickedness. I sit twixt trouble, travail --
double.

Ghazal on the unacceptable

"Which unacceptable poet -- Thomas or cummings -- pissed in the potted palms
On the Rogers' penthouse patio?" My mom couldn't remember. "So
      unacceptable."

Joan had the biggest tits I'd ever seen on an airline heiress and she kept on
Visibly adjusting them. But her *goyish* boyfriend was unemployed. Unacceptable.

In the 90s Sue did coke and brunched at my place constantly. She left teeth
      marks
In my Vermont cheddar cheese. Found *that* in the fridge but no blow!
      Unacceptable.

Cass got caught masturbating one time by the housekeepers. She was staying at
Sven's apt. The cleaners came in as she came on top of the washer. Unacceptable.

Now she fantasizes she is watched by workers in her final jerks of *jouissance*:
A brace of plumbers, porters, doormen all observe the orgasm -- acceptable?

The scumbags Carter knows are all middle class or upper: pill-popping-MD's;
Sex-addict-realtors; drunk Juris Docs; bad, but unbroke brokers. Unacceptable.

At a beachfront office in Laguna Beach I list my pains, my traumas. The shrink
      sighs:
"Stephanie, stop it! This rich-white-privilege self-pity thing is fucking
      unacceptable."

hood again in 5

my name is hood. my
biz is gift baskets. my

name was Rodolpho but my
girl-name is Red. my

mom freaked at the sex change. my
grandma got why i did it though. my

big love is for grandma. my
thought: bring her a basket! my

metro card expired though so my
way to grandma is with my

feet along the street. my
calves are killing me and my

basket slips. who grabs it? my
name is Wolf, says the guy. my

real name is Red, i said. what is mine
became his -- i liked it. oh my.

Tercet Tragedics

He said I looked like her
But I was the nicest, the sweetest
And most importantly RIGHT THERE.

She arrived; he left me. I seduced him with a Paris dress--
He loved me most he said, and he said it in French
Then I went home to New York. I knew I was the best

Woman for him. He said *oui*. We would clinch
The deal in NYC -- Then the telegram came--
I wrote him pages; he wrote back something devastatingly simple.

Just another day of poetic repetition

You were watching the Rays. I was typing
A report or a poem -- I forget. The sun was beating
Down on the urban palms and the heat was driving
Against our windows, full of allergens.

The Santa Anas were driving me crazy. You
Were full of hot urbanized ennui re Baseball. I was sighing
That we hadn't gotten shades for the windows, how
Reports tended to beat out poetry, no matter how I watched

My priorities. The work beat us down and the palm trees
Whipped me into frenzy for clouds. I sighed for pines, not this toxic sunshine;
I'd drive up north all the way to the fog and the rain, but there was
No time for that. There was typing to be done and more baseball. Then daughter
        drove

Up the driveway, sighing. She didn't want to do any more typing
But couldn't help it. None of us could. Can. We are wedded to these keyboards,
        we reek
Of urbanization. I detest palm trees. She is so beat. You fear we are losing.

Devorah and Jael give to the Spenserian (he deserves it [for J. Allyn])

You see me twice -- no three times in the Torah:
First I'm under that stupid palm tree; the commentary
argues, I sit 'cause I don't want the guys to be mad I'm chief -- "Huzzah!"
I say, "I'm the boss!" Dude, I sit under the god-damned (sorry, Adonai) tree
because in case you haven't noticed, it's f***ing hot out here in Judea.
My second appearance is me telling Barak to get off his ass and fight
Sisera's army. He says, "will you go with me?" (Typical). "I might"
I reply back to him. The third time you see me I dance with Jael,
who's nailed a tent hook through Sisera's forehead. That's my kind of gal.

2 anaphora lists

the time that mattered

The time she almost did it. She was naked and 16, and her body didn't
    belong to her, and it was beautiful. She loved to be with it. The
    boy was immaterial. Barely there.
The first time she did it. It hurt like hell. The boy she wanted. Lovely,
    but unknowing. A mess of straining muscles and incredible pain.
The second time the same.
Times 3-7 the same. The doctor he said. The doctor. She went. They
    operated.
The 8th time. Didn't hurt. But something had been lost in the
    transmutation of flesh.
The 9th time -116th the same sort of nothing.
The time she did it with herself. She lay on the tile of the bathroom floor.
    She wasn't sure how to operate the machinery. It was a no go,
    and then.
Suddenly. It went.

Why I love my dishwasher

Because you can put a lot of dishes in it before you have to run it.
Because it's white and black and turquoise and German.
Because it has a nice rack for wine glasses and they don't get smashed.
Because it has a good spot for knives and they don't slip through and get caught
in the mechanism at the bottom.
Because I can pretend to do the dishes, but just barely rinse them and throw
them in there and no one finds out til much later when there's still gunk on them
after the cycle.
Because dishwashers excited my mother and my grandmother who both hated
cleaning and didn't much like to cook.
Because it makes a wishing sound. I mean a whishing sound. But also the first
        thing.
Because when you press yourself against it.... see previous poem.

2 sonnets

When the waves don't work

If my father's house has many mansions, I wonder
How many units my mom's condo has. Sorry. I realize
I'm being obscure. I mean, we think patriarchy has been torn asunder
By 2nd, 3rd and 4th wave feminism's constructions. Their high-rises
Stretch across race and class; yet when I ask you about the history of these
        houses
You act like I'm living in a tenement of worn-out essentialist theories.
There's an architectural disconnect, don't you think? What we mouth
Does not build us or other women up. The words do not retrofit how we
Treat other grrls, bois, trans, and all undecideds. Our lack of kindness has not
        changed
For all this theoretical castle building. We are still housed in untheorized
        bitchery:
The passive aggression of the dissimilarly oppressed, still sharp, still fanged
We hurtle against each other in conversation, and daggered looks:
Raise roofs but demolish shining cities of choices, political acts, possible books.

For my mother

We did not hug or kiss much. We loved most when we shopped.
When I was fat, she bore witness in the dressing room at Saks;
I sobbed and sighed at shorts that would not squeeze on. I mopped
Up the tears. She sat and smiled like the Buddha, accepting. Back
At Schraffts I vowed to lose weight over a hot fudge sundae. "My last
One," I declared. "Maybe," she said. "Maybe not." Then I got thin at camp.
She nodded, agreed it was probably smart, but she herself resisted
Social skinny, sat luxuriant in folds of flesh at Bonwits, as I vamped
Formal wear and blue jeans, coats, shoes, jackets, skirts and I forget what else.
And then the GAP -- when my father died. She sent me there for a purple dress.
"Black is boring," she said. "So expected." Until her last year she pressed
Me to buy "a decent outfit" with her hard earned cash. The final gift felt
Extravagant: A pair of moss green shoes from France. She was generous --
I had forgotten that. Remember now the sizing of the love we shared. Enormous.

2 couple(t)s of academics_

At yesterday's department meeting
I noticed the most peculiar seating;
The husbands arrived quite late; their wives arriving punctual
Because the men were full professors and the dames -- mostly -- adjunctual.

Acrostic: Riverside Calif., 2012

Random exit on the 60, ½ way from Hollywood to Other Desert Cities:
Inland Empire's a nice epithet but we got the most foreclosures in the nation
      here.
Veterinarians hole up in strip malls between a taqueria and an old hospital.
Even the usually chipper Starbucks barristas froth drinks grim and gaunt for the
      few
Raging customers: the 1% of the city, or else the OC high school grads who blew
      the
SAT's and ended up at the campus here instead of UCLA or Santa Barbara.
"I'm transferring," a rich freshman informs me. "And Professor, I'm in a wedding
      the
"Day of the final exam – so I have to take it early or late." "On a Wednesday?" I
      say.
"Eccentric choice for a festivity that people have to travel to." She shrugs a chic
      bag.
Conversely, a student who works 3 jobs and takes care of her baby sister says to
      me
"Am I going to make it through college?" I lend her the books,
Look out at the freeway, where the cars roar past to some drier destination
In the promise of a proper desert with sand and swimming pools and pretty
      vistas
From where I came too, looking for work and arid spaces. I found them, I guess.

Semi-Formal

Sehnsucht: A personal ad

White, near-sighted, tallish Middle-aged Woman who cannot drive, garden, cook, add, subtract, divide, or multiply past 5's seeks younger man of any ethnicity with comfortable car and ample arms for managing shoes, hard copies, and an ill-defined sense of nihilism.

You are funny, smart (entry level genius preferred), kind, and modest, with an ability to tolerate Korean soap operas turned to a very high volume while the gluten free cookies burn in the its-not-my-fault oven. Quiet voice a plus. High fidelity a must.

Do you like Kraft Macaroni And Cheese and anxiety-ridden walks to the post office or pharmacy to pick up packages and pills? Are you a non-smoker who fancies doing taxes while discussing environmental disasters, the two-state solution and the failure of higher education in our time?

If so, I'm your girl.

PS – I can't lie down or bend over for 2 hours after I eat, due to acid reflux. Otherwise, I'm good to go if you know what I mean, and am super flexible for my age, thanks to Pilates and a strict routine of aerobic (but existentially complex and therefore emotionally satisfying) kvetching.

The Dadaists reluctantly choose a form (For John Ashberry)

We are tired of: sound poems, brutist poems, exquisite corpses.
Tonight for one night only, the Café Voltaire in conjunction with
Club Dada declares: The Night of One Thousand Haiku (to be composed
immediately, without recourse to Basho, or to any source --
be it Japanese, Albanian, Swiss–German, or Australian).
Write at your own risk; poetry is dangerous but necessary --
Please pay at the door. All currencies accepted: *domo, danke,* thanks.

Haiku Hebrew (again, for Ashberry)

We're talking Hebrew –– not really; we're reading –– more *attempting* to read
Super slowly- those of us who didn't learn it as kids ––we struggle
To parse the letters; *n* looks like *k* looks like *b*, and the final *mem*
And the final *kaf*, they look completely different in print than in script.
"We're talking Hebrew," Lev says "did you think the ancient tongue would just
      flow?"
"Yes," I say. "I did. I thought it would be simpler. This reading backwards!"
"But it's not backwards, if reading right to left is what you've always known."
"We're talking Hebrew! The language of the Bible! It's so exciting!"
"Yeah, I guess." We squint–– Julie and me –– at the cards the teacher holds up.
"It's – don't tell me – *shem*." "*Tov!*" says the teacher (that means "good" like "*Mazel
      Tov*").
We shrug at *shem*; it means "name" but what of *Yerushalayim*? Oy veh!
There are more long words. And it gets much worse you know. There are no
      vowels
Written in Hebrew. You have to guess them. Know them. The way we're reading
In class is a cheat. You should know the words without seeing the vowels.
Invisible signs, like what Moses saw alone, the faith reflected
In the mystery of words, both seen and unseen. We're talking Hebrew ––
Kaballah lingo, the characters of Tarot, alphabet of fire.
The Mystics thought if you could read the Torah right, you could reinvent
Paradise through language, bring the Messianic Age to earth right now.
We're talking Hebrew, which sounds like this: *anachnu medabrim ivrit*.

Almost sonnet about oatmeal

It's the last of the oatmeal but it's all right I think -- we have more
or at least enough for tomorrow. . . maybe just barely enough for 1 person
And then -- nothing for it -- I'll have to walk back again to the store.
What? I hate grocery shopping; there were 3 guys at that bus bench in the sun
asking for money-- they made me feel guilty because I have so much
more than they do (so much more than so many, but I still want more of it) --
Okay, I'll buy milk too, and eggs, and cheese, and yes the oatmeal – which
brand do you like? I can't remember. I just don't want to face those bits
of broken manhood at the bus stop. "You have a nice day" I said to one guy
idiotically, and he said "you too," but I feel like he was being sarcastic. How
could he not be and what the fuck was I thinking wishing this and why
did I say it? I genuinely wished him well but couldn't open my purse to show
my wallet. My mother said *never do that in public*. Oatmeal, mouthwash, and milk
while we're at it. And some courage? Perhaps. But no less guilt.

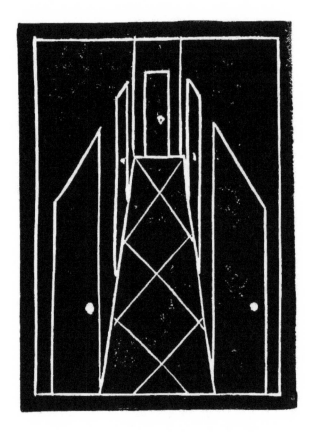

Memo to the Factory of Tears (for Valzhyna Mort)

To: the Factory of Tears Collective
From: Management
Re: Benefits -- fiscal, political, metaphysical and misc (i.e. Items not categorized
under the forgoing Rubrics)

1. The Management has received your Requests.

2. Management met with the Board of Directors
In high-rise Buildings overlooking the Boulevards
Of Bonds, above the squalid Investments which Management
Avoids mostly through the use of special Elevators and
Limousines waiting outside a secret Exit at the Back, near the Garbage Cans.

3. We deliberated, which means talked. We had Luncheon
Sent in and then Dinner. We billed many Hours.

4. We have concluded the Following:
      4.a. the Answer is
No.
      4.b. A detailed Report of this No -- its Whys, Wherefores, and Futures
(along with substantial
Graphs, Images, and Forecasts of why No matters and why No is right)
will be made available
In a few Months or Years.
      4.c. Employees may use their Security Clearance to access
The --
(Message truncated due to Size)

Ottava non-rima per noi (for us)

I have come home from a trip and things are not "right" between
"Us." The mother–daughter "thing" -- there is no adequate word for
Its tangle; the emotions are strange: bedeviled, blessed, both. Neither. My
       mother,
My mother -- well-what can I say about *that*? What non–pronounced syllables
       can
Elaborate the sense of "absent"? So I try to break that chain of pain (as I
Named it to my first therapist) with my daughter, and it works well
Mostly. But then it doesn't. Right now we sit at the kitchen table
Each with laptops as something unmentionable reeks rotten under windows

Of silence. When things are "good" between me and her there is enchantment--
Laughter licks the wind of words and more love than you can shake any kind of
Stick at -- divining rod, magic wand, or peace pipe --vibrates the vocal cords.
       But
Sometimes, there is this awful quiet. The wordlessness of women who cannot
       speak
Their minds or guts. The abject something that sticks in the craw between
The generations. The envy, the impatience –the I wish you were dead but
Dare not say so translated into poisonous glances over tables that have gone
On for years -- O the wish to be free of the looks of women: my mother,

My daughter, or that former best friend whom I fear now but once dearly loved
Until she said at a holiday party that my daughter really resembled HER--was
Consequently HER daughter (she claimed my kid under the Christmas tree, as
her *real* daughter and I groaned, gripping melting menorah candles). Now my
Former friend erupts in these strange annunciations; she phones my husband,
       says
We should be neighbors or should share a big house like in Dynasty or Dallas.
       That's
Crazy shit. But it's how I feel about my daughter --I wish she'd live here always
       though
We are sitting here just now baleful in the kitchen. There is something rotten in

The state of this love that transforms too fast into fingers tapping on the coffee
Cup with a traitorous transmission: Why did you come back at all? This is my
House now. Watch out, though: final quiet comes when you least
Expect it. You were 8, playing with a friend one December, when my mother
       phoned

(I'd stopped telling her anything substantial after I slept with that Italian boy
        and
She told me –– albeit indirectly–– I was a whore). We settled for a linguistic sort
        of
Blankness, talked in trivialities. But I remember that last conversation.
"I'm scared," she said "I'm scared and I feel so stupid." I tried for a modicum

Of sympathy ––dredged up a little–– but I had to hang up and watch the kids.
        She
Died that weekend in her chair over breakfast, the apartment manager told
Me later. The point is this: We have got to grenade these guilty half–phrases. I
        want
My mother back, and I want you to stay. I want all our love unvarnished,
Uncontained, unrepentant. I want to sit with you at this stupid fucking table
        and
Remember your grandmother and even my terrifying former girlfriend's terrifying
Mater, and all our other crazy bitch relations. Imperfectly articulate. Struggling
Against the sentence and the strictured articulation. Stammering You. Me. Us.

Woman to woman (for Alan Dann)

A woman came up to me in Bloomingdales and said she liked my glasses and I told her where to get them and she said, "what do you think I am-- a millionaire?" and stomped off.

A woman came up to me in grad school and said she wished she was as smart as I was and I told her where to find the good theory books at the library and she said 'what do you think I am-- stupid or something?" and threw down her copy of Derrida's On Grammatology and stomped off.

A woman came up to me in the airport in Montpellier and said "Ce livre -- De La Grammatologie par Derrida -- c'est à vous?" and I told her I had picked it up off the ground in North Carolina, and the woman said' Quoi? Vous êtes un connard Americain?" and lit a Gauloise and stomped off.

A woman came up to me in the hospital and said "this is your baby," and I took the baby, but she said, "I can tell already you're a terrible mother," and threw the baby blankets at my husband and stomped off.

A woman came up to me at the swimming pool and wanted to know why my 2 year old daughter was laughing at her classmate, and I explained that she had never seen a penis before, and the woman said "DON'T USE THAT FOUL WORD IN MY PRESENCE," threw a beach ball at my head, and stomped off.

A woman came up to me at my house and said she wondered what all these little girls were doing, drawing with chalk on the driveway, and I said they were friends of my daughter and she said "YOUR CHILDREN ARE OUT OF CONTROL," and the girls started laughing, and they all took giant steps behind her as she stomped off.

A woman came up to me at the university and said she wondered why everyone was so mean to each other on campus, and I said "what do I look like – a therapist?", and she said "actually, yes, you do," and stomped off.

A woman came up to me at a shopping mall entrance, and gave me a Kleenex because I was crying into the telephone fighting with my husband, and I said "thank you" and she said "don't mention it; I know how you feel. You just wish you could stomp off."

A woman came up to me at the Northampton bus station, and she said she knew me from somewhere, and I said "I am your mother," and she said "I know--I'm just kidding and being weird!" and then she laughed and pretended to stomp off.

A woman came up to me on the beach and she said she knew where all the magic stones were, and I put down my copy of Derrida, and laid out a beach blanket, and we took turns stomping off and looking for magic rocks and then bringing them back, lying on the blanket, telling each other stories, while wearing each other's sunglasses.

Sestina (fake) for Chrysler, my father, and me

here's the deal:
Chrysler, who has always made shitty cars
is avoiding bankruptcy;
creditors are screaming
about the gap
in $$ but it's all preliminary, folks.

the deal is this:
you can hate Chrysler all you want
but their bankruptcy means ours
and our <u>own</u> creditors screaming down our backs:
the GAP will fold, and so will Banana Republic
and the preliminary mortgage you thought you had-- gone.

no fucking deal, you say.
let Chrysler fold.
let the companies that deserve bankruptcy go under.
may the creditors sell the damned furniture from under
those gap-teethed CEO's.
Hang 'em high, and that's just a prelim

to what I'd like to do to them--bankrupt those bastards
from Chrysler and Wall Street,
playing with our money like this was a Monopoly tournament
and a preliminary one at that.
if I were a creditor I'd shut them down in an instant
that's the deal I'd offer.

I tell my husband this, as we mend the gap in the ceiling and walls;
our house is collapsing, but we don't have any credit.
I look down the driveway at my father's Chrysler.
buy American he said but he declared bankruptcy
so many times, it became a game-- always preliminary, never definitive--
it's no way to live he told me, but that's the deal I've made

he said, so don't get poor if you can help it, don't declare bankruptcy--
it tears gaps in your soul you can never fix
and if you buy Chrysler be sure to get the extended warranty;
the creditors don't care what you thought or what you hoped.
there is no dealing with them in emotions
(this speech was always a preliminary move before the booze came out).

so, I've made some preliminary decisions: I will not declare bankruptcy;
I'll give Dad's Chrysler to the handyman so he can fix the ceiling; I will
have no creditors;
I will not deal in gaps, spiritual or otherwise.

Informal

Doll Defenestration

I did it.
I threw the dolls out the window
Why?
Because it suited me and I was the queen of all I
Surveyed in the bedroom:
The child's toy chest, the wooden chairs, the tea set.
The grown up stuff was mummy's and what was left was dad's.

The rubber prince was the first to go.
He squeaked strangely;
Away with ye I said.
Then went Carrots who was a midsize girl with red
Hair –
A shy foolish thing, and *so begone* --
And the Madame Alexander dolls:
Queen Elizabeth, Heidi,
And all 4 of the Little Women.

They all went for one reason or another,
Chasing Peter Pan,
Moonbeams,
Or because I JUST DIDN'T LIKE 'EM but had to say I
Did
'cause I was most polite being an only child
And a descendent of the Romanovs
Meaning you always had to say thank you
For gifts you didn't like
And also you bled a lot-- potentially.

But I came a cropper
When my mother found them all on the window sill of
My grandfather's studio
2 floors below our place.

The moral of this story is:
Watch out for your grandparents

They are always lurking around
And they will get you into trouble because
They have old fashioned sharp eyes that go out and
In like telescopes
That see odd tiny forms out the window at night
And they'll show them to your mother who will
Know then that you throw away your dolls like some
Brash bratty Bolshevik
And she'll comb their hair with silver teeth
Plucked from the jaws of her patent leather purse,
Wearing pearls, a disgusted expression and
Suddenly scary
Enamel
Painted eyes.

Kenny

Kenny has gap teeth;
He works at an old age home
He changes diapers and takes people to
The park.
He wanted to talk to me on
The metrolink.
I'm old too I told him
When he gave me his number
And asked what I was reading
While in the seats behind me his cousin
And his cousin's friends
Yelled pussy and penis and
I'll tape her mouth shut.
I'm a one-man soldier
The cousin said at one point.
He's staying with me said
Kenny. He shrugged.
Family.

Reading Václav Havel's obituary

It began with Czechoslovakia:
I was green 13 at camp in New Hampshire
and I saw the Life photos
Of the tanks rolling in. Something
Changed in me. Something rose up.
Then in New York with you in our 30s
At the Public. Theater: the play Havel wrote
About the brewery. The intellectual stood
Not understanding beer, till the manager
Taught him how to chug a big glass. The play
Shocked me somehow--I couldn't chug on a bet--
I looked at your leg crossed over
The other in the theater, and saw
The holes in your shoes.
Later, on a cold walk you explained to me --
How the two men
Drinking beer together at the end --
That meant something --
Intellectuals need to understand regular people
Learn from them even --
Do what they do. There is wisdom in daily habits
A generosity in the smallest gesture --
that elites don't understand.
This statement mystified me for years. Til once
At Disneyland I helped a child
Release her foot from some grillwork. She had stuck it through
And panicked.
I saw how to pull her out.
Děkuji, said the father. You are Czech?,
I said in English,
But he had already
Turned away. This means,
I think, now as I read Havel's
Obituary-- that the work is never done. The intellectual
Bends under unending
Obligation. You've helped once? --big deal!

56

Says the Brewer. You've understood one person?
How about a thousand? A million? More?
The theater's fine, but the challenge of the tanks
Remains:
how to deal with them once they've come, and how
--ideally--
to keep them
From ever coming.

Eve

her new self
strips its skin
like a snake.
the cold air
feels greenly crisp, apple moist
to
a serpent woman who
sloughs off the garden
sidewinds her way to
a
wilder
freedom.

old chocolate

chocolate left
too long in the glove compartment
it crumbled in my hand
outside faded to a flaky ash
soft inside – a sad dead sweet
I ate it anyway
and wrote these words
on the back of
my father's will
which lay on the passenger seat
for more than a year.

Sister Sabbath

When you light the candles you are never alone:
Anne Frank and Anna Freud leave off writing with the setting sun
Deborah leaves her swords by the door
Wields twin braids of bread instead
While
Ruth sets the table
Esther pours the wine, and Emma
Goldman (though not a believer)
Intones the blessing
To honor the sisters who
Stand by their chairs as the others come
Behind them and
Glimmer in the dark like flickering lights:
Housewives and rabble--rousers
Sweatshop workers, prophets
Prostitutes, queens, mavens, movie stars
And
Camp survivors
Clasping mothers, daughters, aunts, and nieces
And all who did not survive--
These come too
      Pouring through the
                Door like smoke
                            From the cinders

                    and on their heels

          the new ones enter

    their unborn faces lit by stars.

Kindred all
You call them simply
When you strike the match
And kindle the lights.

Epistle to the Hebrews -- reboot

Dear Hebrews:
How Pharoah loved you.
You worked so hard
Built so much, and retreated to your secret houses
Where you keep your secret ways. All that lamb's
Blood. All that flat
Bread. And you told such
Stories! Boys in rainbow coats and women giving
Birth at 80 or 90. You interpreted dreams and your women
Were beautiful and industrious. Imagine, how
Pharaoh must have
Felt! Losing his best workers to a series of unfortunate
Events. Imagine how he fought that destiny. How he
Sent out armies. Think how our own
Hearts harden because we love too
Desperately--with too little suppleness. Like stone when we should be
Water
Carrying Moses in his basket to the fluid princess. Yet water doesn't always
Work. In the end, the miraculous
Child becomes a mumbling murderer with a god-awful temper who
Talks to enflamed hedges and calls forth frogs and death and then pulls the
          whole
Work Force out after
Tremendous suffering. Talk about a brain
Drain! Talk about Insult and Injury! But even then Pharaoh
Grieved. The waters
Opened, closed and here we all are on opposing
Shores. Now you pick up the ark as he
Lays down that crown, that heavy
Helmet of empire. You'll decide you want a king and he'll decide that
Being Pharoah was only
Good while the Jews were there. So now, we'll all be someone else's
Entirely. Walk the perimeters of our as yet unnamed countries where we
Harbor--
The suspicion that
We are never masters of our domain. Only its inhabitants. Not even that--
Visitors, travelers, wanderers along the narrow channels that we must

Now stop to taste. Bending and cupping our hands, bringing them quickly to
Our lips before the water can run through, sucking each
Finger like a reed.

It's all in the vowels

I would love to live in Paris no, not
Perris-- hey, that reminds me of
When Ryan first started teaching here at Poly
He said in the lunchroom, gee Lacie
Look at all the kids from Paris
Funny--they don't SOUND French at all
And I said for Christ's sake Ry,
There's no one from fucking France here, trust me
They mean P–E–R–R–I–S
Not P–A–R–I–S

As in the Lake? He said, and I said
Yah!
Oh, he said, oooooohhhhhhh
But then we went to the Alpha Beta after I coached the chess club and he
Led band practice
And pretended to be at the *marché aux* something
The vegetable one, not *puces,* --that means
Fleas.
We acted very fluttery and waved our hands puffed out
Our cheeks and acted surprised and resigned
At the strange goings on zee–how–do–yu–say–eet? Inland Empire

We said *merci* to the checkout girl with
The thick glasses and
The scary bagger boy with his skinhead
Slump and his murderkiller
I've–spotted–a–kike–and–a–queer–in–line–together eyes--
The one, who, as we left
Murmured *Au revoir, monsieur-dame.*

Torah Bones

listen:
cradled for the first time in these arms
there is a clicking of sticks
a soft settling of joints.

all ribs, spines, and shanks
this curious body's ungainly
cumbersomely easy to hold a
strange
ancient child
whose flesh is
texts.

In a bad way or Foucault said it (for Robert Van Cleave)

He's in a bad way, the doctor said to me
And right then I knew my dad wasn't going to make graduation--
Professor, I knew he was going to fight and go down and never see me get
         hooded--
Which he'd always wanted--the first PhD in the family.

You see he was in such a bad way-- and not just from the cancer--
He hated how the staff all treated him

Like a laboratory animal, some caged dumb creature Not
Fully alive. He was in a really bad way but he noticed all of the horrid
Things the nurses do--like letting you wet yourself and lie in your piss for
Hours.
They sashay past going to get coffee as you push the fucking--excuse me--
Bell.
It was like-- remember when we studied Michel Foucault?
And you said Foucault said
"the prison, the hospital, the school, the army are systems that make you
into a docile body, a docile mind that obeys conforms surrenders accepts."
Well my dad **got** all that, and it made him so **crazy** to be the object of
Their knowledge, their stinking I don't give a damn if you live or
Die protocol that he cursed
The nurses whenever they went by
Till one of them was in such a bad way that
She ran in tears to me over in the waiting room.

You're his son, she sobbed.
Can't you talk to him?
Tell him to stop that.
But when I tried to explain what he really needed, her eyes glazed over.
So Professor in the end I couldn't even help him, and he was in a real
Bad way--hooked up to all those tubes and it was ugly and awful and
Something bigger than
Sad.
But right before the end, he took my hand and said fiercely Son,
I LOVE you
While with the other he gave the doctor and the nurses
A final
Fuck you finger.

To the IRS

My mother will not be paying her taxes this year
She died 3 years ago actually
And therefore I don't think she owes you anything more
Than what she's already paid you
Out of her monthly salary checks which were quite small

She worked until the day she died
Dropped dead waiting for the bus
At the corner of 73rd and Lex

I'm not complaining about how little she left me
But I don't think she's in arrears or beholden or behind with you people

So please clear her account
Or whatever you call it
Over there where you are.

Formless

Boxes and Bags

T. lives in a small house filled with boxes. The boxes come from France, Los Angeles, and Gloversville, NY. The house is in Riverside, CA. It is near the river, but you can't see it from the windows or even from the street. You know it is there, though.

The boxes have pens, post-its that are purple, pink, yellow and blue, little plastic boxes to keep the stuff in when she unpacks it, and a lot of sheets and towels. The linens belonged to her mother before she died, and now T. thinks she will keep it all, in case she gets a condo in Los Angeles. She gets lonely in Riverside and she still has cousins and some friends in the city.

There are also a lot of bags on the floor in T.'s house. The bags hold the books that she can't fit onto the bookshelves. She has a lot of books. They are triple stacked on the bookshelves, and piled on 3 of the kitchen chairs, the left half of the sofa in the living room, and on the desk chair in her room. She reads a lot, because she is a historian.

T.'s mother never finished high school but she liked to hear about the things that T. knew. Her name was M. and she came from Russia.

When I come from Los Angeles to visit T. says please don't mind the mess and I say no, not at all I do not mind. She says I will get this organized one day and I say not on my account. She says my mother and I say my mother too. I have bags of fancy cloth napkins that I got from my mother's apartment when she died. They stayed in a group near my bed til my husband got mad and made me move them. I like them there I said.

They've got to go, he said to me. He meant business.

So I took them out of the bags and I folded them up and I put them in an old Saks 5th Avenue box that my mother had her pearls in and I put the napkins on the top shelf of my hall closet. Sometimes I take them out and smell them, and then I fold them up and put them away near the stacks of blue covered yearbooks, the oak box holding the silverware, and the Bloomingdale's shopping bag filled with black and white photographs of my mother and her mother, who--like M. --was from Russia. Bathed in light, they look like movie stars. Looking out beyond their 40s lipstick and waved hair. I take them out and look back at them, holding their mementos, carrying their genes, the dna wrapped in packages tied with bright chromosome ribbons.

Encased in boxes of bones, bags of organs, the slippery sacks of skin.

2 About East Germany

Berlin Fragment/Berlinfragment: 1974

I have started learning German at college, because my
boyfriend speaks it, and he says real intellectuals speak German.

He is doing a junior year in Hamburg and he has become a
Marxist.

I have become a feminist.

I visit him for Christmas.

We fight a lot.

My boyfriend insists that we go to a place that I know as
East Berlin.

"DON'T call it that," he says. "It's *Berlin Hauptstadt der DDR*."

"What does that mean?" I say.

He says "it means 'Berlin, capital of the German Democratic
Republic.'"

I say "Oh."

My boyfriend has just informed me that he now has a
German girlfriend that he is seeing when I'm not around, and I feel
pretty mad. I look up the word for "mad" in my pocket English-
German dictionary.

The word is *böse*.

We take the train from Hamburg to West Berlin. My
boyfriend insists that we cross the border into Berlin *Hauptstadt der
DDR*– not through Checkpoint Charlie (which is how most
Americans go) -- but through some train station where real
Germans go.

The border crossing = nightmare.

The officials make you sit in a waiting room, and they call
your passport numbers individually. My boyfriend's number is
called and he disappears. I sit and sit. The problem is that when the
guy calls my number he says "TZVO" and not "TZVEI" (for the
number "two"). So, I don't understand.

Finally, a soldier comes in and yells at me. I get through, and my boyfriend is embarrassed because I'm such an idiot American. I am freaked out by this experience, and all the books by Marx in the bookstores freak me out too. But I eat the only decent meal I get in Germany during that trip to Berlin Hauptstadt der DDR. Fish at a restaurant in a tower, where we have to wait an hour to get in.

My boyfriend buys me <u>Das Kapital</u> translated into English. I never read it.

Thinking of East Germans in Los Angeles on the bus

As East Germans my two friends were poignant and heroic;
she was a doctor and he was an editor. Then the wall fell and they
wanted washing machines, small portable cameras, and cell phones
--they ate at MacDonald's and vacationed in Palm Springs. It was
crazy how fast they adapted to capitalism; they ran around
Universal Studios and raved about the steaks. I skulked along with
them, nostalgic for their soviet-made Brabant car, the Czech beer
we drank in the Prenzlauer Berg and sf poems about cosmonauts
making friends with folks from Mars. We fell out of touch. Last I
heard they were living in a big house on the German/Dutch border.
I sit on the 704 rapid bus and think about how much I liked East
Berlin: how great the transportation was and how you didn't have
to have a car to get around the city. The subway ran all night--and
there were young single moms working important jobs with lots of
little children, and there weren't any people living on the street.

Across from me a man offers to help a woman with her bags
for 10 dollars. I got to get paid, he tells her. She says if I had that
kind of money I'd take a goddamned cab.

Madness in the Method

1.
You have no method Miss Von Heerman told me in Latin
class. Your translations are correct but you can't explain them. I
knew nothing about artistic intuition so I thought she was telling
me what most teachers told me--that I was stupid. Also lazy. No
method meant many things including no college. You'll never be
accepted my principal told me in front of my beautifully dressed
bankrupt parents.

2.
You have no theoretical approach, honey, my graduate advisor told
me my first semester as a Ph.D. candidate. I hated him even on the
day he called me his most brilliant student at the airport while my
stunned dissertation director smiled uncomprehendingly (he was
German). Later I learned that my advisor's entire family was
hanged in the town square in Czechoslovakia. They all resisted
Hitler. I hated him anyway.

3.
There is no method to knowledge in the human sciences Hans
Georg Gadamer writes. I read his books on the flight to my father's
funeral. My dad lost his job at 50 and never worked again. He broke
his hip but I know it was his heart that broke first. We learn from
experience, Gadamer says, and most experiences are--by their very
nature--dangerous, and often negative.

Skulls

There are too many skulls. The Koreans say so, and the Germans say so, and the Sudanese say so, and some Israelis and some Palestinians--mostly women--say so too. There are too many skulls say the children in Chile. Too many say the homeboys in Moreno Valley. But what else is there here in America? Or in the world?" I'll tell you what else say the women in black, I'll tell you what else say the widows in Oaxaca, in Belfast, in Brooklyn, in Bangladesh, in Homs. There is something else.

But what is it, want to know the men in charge and sometimes the women medals clanking and power suits set to high stun. *We'll have to do a study of whatever it is or might be, form a sub-committee, have a discussion and file a report and then a roundtable, a seminar, and maybe even a conference, before we can actually do anything with whatever it is. You see we have to be logical, we have to be careful, and so we will pile up the skulls in a perfect pyramid, while we think and talk and discuss and debate what might be better, what might be else, than these white shining faces, their eyes empty and knowing with smiles that are silent, which is probably best.*

Shall I? (For e.e. cummings and Bill Shakespeare)

Shall I say how darling the buds of May are even though it's April and it's Los Angeles, and there are no frigging buds here unless they are tended by underpaid gardeners and overpaid landscapers and a bunch of sprinklers?

Shall I talk about this pretty how town? Shall I say that it's pretty darned temperate now, but in September and October it's awfully hot? That the kids sweat in their Halloween costumes and sometimes it's too hot to carve the Thanksgiving turkey? Shall I admit that I love my pretty how town even though both Shakespeare and cummings wouldn't like it, since one was a Brit and the other was an east coast Harvard man? Shall I say that John Fante and Joni Mitchell and Occupy and the Radical Fairies and the Zoot Suiters found LA compelling even though it wasn't (and isn't) darling? Shall I say that from where I sit I can see helicopters and the Hollywood sign and old school street lamps and a surprising tree and I can hear the kids at the school next door yelling far and wheeeeeee? That's from another cummings poem, but I like him, and I like Shakespeare too, so I'll compare thee, Los Angeles to thyself. Aka yourself. And say I dig you.

Palavas

Palavas, near Montpellier, is like the Bronx, if your squint your eyes and think hard enough. We are leaning on cars watching French Punks go by and tough looking dogs follow them home and the sun is setting, and we're going to a party perhaps or going our separate ways because this is France and I am young and you are younger. I watch you walk across the street. You make a phone call with your friend and you're hanging out of the phone booth the receiver against your ear and your face is asking urgently for something and your hand gestures towards me, and I wait for the cars to go by, so I can cross over and we can make our plans: catch a bus, or get a ride with the person on the phone, or with someone else, because we don't have a car, and anyway, I don't know how to drive.

Smile American

The cafeteria in Geneva is filled with an international crowd, where everyone looks like something else. The Germans look like Italians, and the Arabs all look French, the Swedes dig the Beatles, and the Spanish all play jazz. Africans don't look African- American but rather English or Canadian. Only I am what I appear in a practical short haircut and a crisp white-girl North Carolina dress. Is Reagan president yet? Maybe not. All I know is I have to defend a country that is already pretty indefensible. In a foreign language. So all I can do is. Smile from ear to ear.

Ars Judaica

1

    I see the word *holocaust* and I have to read whatever it is. I am Norwegian on one side, Russian on the other. The wrong kind of Russian, meaning the horrid horrible Romanovs or perhaps it is the right kind, if you are in to Fabergé eggs and murder. I belong to the ancestors who persecuted your ancestors I tell my husband, who chased you over the frozen wastes of Russia. Only in America he says, smiling. He kisses me and I can taste the liverwurst and pumpernickel and the strong calves of people who know how to run. All on his tongue. He tastes like survival.

2

    You look Jewish she says. You don't look Jewish another one says. My friend's parents whisper anti-Semitic jokes, when I am at their house. Is she. . . ? they say to each other. NO, I say loudly, but I am filled with the fury of the Cohen (the priestly class) over this slight. I am 17. My boyfriend's name is Sy Metzger He is regrettably very tight with money. But a thing of beauty to look at. A brilliant filmmaker, a passable lover.

3

    I pass all the time, or try to. Jewish/not Jewish. The women seem to know. But not always. Janie Glick – my roommate at college-- invited me to her house and her father told his sisters I kept kosher. They looked at me and beamed. Of course they said of course. Louis Glick winked at me, and offered me a cigar. Gertrude Stein smoked them I say. The sisters are still smiling.

4

8 years old. I go out to Long Island to see a house my Romanov grandparents are considering buying. The lunch that we get is borscht out of a thermos. What IS this? Red stuff-- it's Russian. I absolutely hate it. However, I will come to love gefilte fish and bagels. A paradox. How can you not love borscht? my mother in law asks. It's so Russian.

5

How I love Jewish men, my mother said. She dated a Jewish guy seriously. Even met his parents. In the Merchant Marine. During the war. He came into town, and they stayed out so late he missed his train. She directed him to a hotel. Oh my god, said my mother. I looked at my girl friend who came with us. And realized the hotel was restricted. They all were. She sighed. I felt so terrible. I said what's restricted?

6

Goddamn Jews, said my father. But he had a huge nose, yelled and used his hands. Self-hating Jew, a lot of Jews must have thought. But no, he was a self-hating Norwegian. What's the difference? Oy.

7

I convert. My mother is furious. I feel cheated, she said. My father is dead and she's an atheist. You're with THEM now, she says. I wonder if she means my husband's family, the Jews in general, or something entirely different. I decide it's the last thing, and I never speak to her again about what moves me. She dies. I say Kaddish for her. Which I'm sure pisses her off.

8

   According to orthodox Rabbis I'm not really Jewish. I find
this oddly comforting. If another Holocaust comes, I can go to the
gas, feeling slightly superior, knowing I have chosen the showers,
not had them chosen for me.

9

   I find equilibrium of sorts in German. My mother and my
Romanov grandmother spoke German. My father in law *is* German,
and he tells me in a fragmented *Muttersprache* about his childhood
years under Hitler. I have the same birthday as Adolph he says and
he will repeat this story many times: his mother lies to him when
he is a small boy on his birthday. She says the swastika flags raised
at the racetrack have in fact been raised for him, in his honor of his
Geburtstag.

   Schau durchs Fenster she tells him in every version. *Look through
the window.* This reminiscence is whispered at the dinner table,
while the family sits stunned by the speaking of the enemy's killer
tongue. Said over and over, *Schau durchs Fenster* sews itself into
memory, an insistent scrap of something that must in turn be told.

Transformative

Excerpts from the Manic Maven Commentary on Maimonides' _Book of_ [613] _Commandments_ (_Sefer Hamitzvot_ [ספר המצוות {originally published in Arabic: _Kitab al-Farai'd}})

Maimonides, Mitzvah 9:
To listen to the prophet speaking in His Name — Deut. 18:15

Manic Maven:
Listen to the appropriate Democrat, Green Party Member, or progressive Liberal in your district, unless that person has been convicted of a felony, has had bathroom sex with a page, has had internet sex with an intern, or has been involved with a suspicious hedge fund. Good Luck.

Maimonides, Mitzvah 10:
Not to try the LORD unduly — Deut. 6:16

Manic Maven:
Don't test your elected officials unduly. It's hard being under public scrutiny ALL the time. Don't give your teachers a tough time either. They are totally underpaid by the way, and really, what have you done for THEM lately?

Maimonides, Mitzvah 11:
To emulate His ways — Deut. 28:9

Manic Maven:
A knock off is a knock off people say, but a classy knock off is an emulation, and a superlative knock off is what certain fancy schmancy New Yorker critics call an _homage_ (pronounced HO-maaj). Now you know. So when someone asks you if your Louis

Vuitton bag is real, you answer, "In a way; it's an *HOMAGE* to the tradition."
You're welcome.

Maimonides, Mitzvah 12:
To cleave to those who know Him — <u>Deut. 10:20</u>

Manic Maven:
Question: Have you cleaved to someone you love today? Doesn't that someone need a good cleaving to? Don't you? So go to that office, school, backyard, hospital room, or bedroom and cleave. Not in the bathroom though--that could be misunderstood. Unless you are expressly invited.

Maimonides, Mitzvah 13:
To love other Jews — <u>Lev. 19:18</u>

Manic Maven:
This is actually a tall order. Because let's face it, other people— and in particular people who are like us — drive us flipping crazy. It's easier to love strangers, because they are different and at least potentially mysterious. But other Jews — not so much. Still, as the song from HAIR goes, don't be hard on the people you're close to, even though, as we know, it's much easier (and more satisfying) to be hard on them.

Maimonides, Mitzvah 14:
To love converts — <u>Deut. 10:19</u>

Manic Maven:

Well, it's certainly easier at the outset to love converts. My husband says he found me most sexually attractive right after I converted, because I was both a *shiksa* and a Jew — and that was tantalizing. Then he realized I was a Jew who couldn't cook, as well as a Jew who insisted on buying retail at places like Nordstrom. What can I tell you? Loving the convert is tricky. But on the other hand, a convert is usually open to kink, and that is worth something in the sack (see #12 on cleaving).

Maimonides, Mitzvah 15:
Not to hate fellow Jews — <u>Lev. 19:17</u>

Manic Maven:

This reminds me of a funny story. When I was interning at J. Laughsalot, a retail store on Madison and 49th, the owners — feuding Egyptian Jewish cousins — refused to pay the bill they owed CUTE HEELS. The cousins hid in their offices whenever the CUTE HEELS rep came by. One time, the rep just strode past me and the other office folks, pounded on the office door, and shouted "I KNOW YOU'RE IN THERE MORTY," to which Morty (somewhat whimsically) responded, "Saul, I'm not here," to which Saul replied "IT'S BECAUSE OF JEWS LIKE YOU THERE WAS HITLER."

The moral of the story is that you shouldn't talk like that to a fellow Jew even if that Jew owes you money and is hiding in their office. How you stop *feeling* mad that they haven't paid you (and are hiding from you and what is more, *letting you know they are hiding from you*) is a more complicated procedure, but that's for you and your therapist to work through.

Maimonides, Mitzvah 16:
To reprove a sinner — <u>Lev. 19:17</u>

Manic Maven:

Interesting. This certainly is connected to what we've been talking about in the previous mitzvah. Elaine Macintosh — my first therapist — argued that you had to confront people who acted badly by saying something like: "What you just did (hide in your office and not pay me and act whimsical about it while I'm pounding on the office door) is something that I experience as extremely hurtful and inadequate." And then see what the other person does. If nothing else, she says, you'll get it out of your system, and you'll "name" the reality and this is empowering. You still may not get paid, but at least the injustice has been made public.

Alternatively, you call a collection agency.

Then you call your lawyer.

Maimonides, Mitzvah17:
Not to embarrass others — <u>Lev. 19:17</u>

Manic Maven:

I don't know about you, but I've been told on several occasions that I'm embarrassing. I tend to talk very loudly at parties, and share things I'm proud of that someone at the party (honoree, fellow guest, spouse, co-worker, child, friend, former student) has done, that they may not want to share or that they have told me in confidence. I can't bring up any specifics, because that would be embarrassing to them, and would do once again this thing that people say I do. So let's just say this: think before you speak, and think before you tell your BFF to jump up on the table where the birthday cake is and show everyone what she's learned in her part-time job as middle-aged pole-dancer.

Maimonides, Mitzvah 18:
Not to oppress the weak — Ex. 22:21

Manic Maven:
Please do NOT:
- Pay less than minimum wage.
- Disrespect union workers.
- Say things like "for this kind of money I'm expecting—" and then name something unreasonable or extra.
- Yell in English at the top of your lungs when the person who works for you does not speak English as their native language.
- Ignore family and friends who are ill. Call them up. Visit, if you can.
- Assume that, because a person is in a wheelchair, they are somehow LESS than you.
- Assume that because someone is a different size or shape than you that they have a moral failing and/or are "unhealthy."
- Assume that because someone has a mood disorder that they are self-indulgent and selfish.
- Ignore the fact that you are probably much richer, whiter, and more privileged than many people, and start behaving with a little humility for Pete's sake.

Maimonides, Mitzvah 19:
Not to speak derogatorily of others — Lev. 19:16

Manic Maven:
Ok, this is a tough one. Or is it? Take this test: Meet a friend for a latte, or a cocktail or a massage and try gossiping about a mutual acquaintance. How do you feel? Better? I bet you feel kind of weird — nervous and high-strung and like you need a

whole other cocktail or massage to calm down (or you regret drinking that caffeinated latte). So resist the urge to gossip. People may still talk smack about YOU, but at least you've left that circle of mean-ness, and your massage will be more luxurious, and that cocktail will taste better.

And maybe switch to decaf, while you're at it.

Maimonides, Mitzvah 20:
Not to take revenge — <u>Lev. 19:18</u>

Manic Maven:

Revenge is stupid. Literature is filled with examples of revenge going wrong from Orestes and Electra to the Count of Monte Cristo. Wait, I think the Count's vengeance works out ok, but that's a French novel, and let's face it, what works for the French, doesn't work for anyone else. I mean, who but Coco really looks good in a Chanel suit? Trying to get revenge on someone is like trying to squeeze into that pencil skirt at Saks while the snooty fitting room lady shakes her head at you. Nope. It's never going to fit. Nastiness makes your legs look short. Not to mention your soul.

Maimonides, Mitzvah 21:
Not to bear a grudge — <u>Lev. 19:18</u>

Manic Maven:

The primary grudge-holders in our society are, in no particular order:
Germanists
Police Officers
Cultural Studies experts
3rd grade girls
Principals' offices
Big Law Firms (particularly the "progressive" ones)

Politicians of all stripes
Germanists

Generally you hold a grudge when you know you can't get revenge on the person and remain out of jail and/or what happened to you is so weird and so personal that you can't explain it to anyone else without their thinking you are a) crazy or b) extremely crazy. When you can't even tell your therapist what happened, because h/she won't understand it either — that's when the grudge sets in. Grudgery also tends to occur in highly bureaucratized/hierarchical settings, which is why there are alot of grudges in hospitals, universities, law firms, government agencies, and schools. This is why when I personally had a disagreement with someone at my fancy schmancy private girls school — I just knocked them down.

And here I am today, totally grudge-free. (although I DID [eventually] have to apologize)

Maimonides, Mitzvah 22:
To learn Torah — <u>Deut. 6:7</u>

Manic Maven:
The question here is: which translation/adaptation of this complex amalgam of texts to learn and teach? There's the *Heart of Darkness* version, and there's the *Portnoy's Complaint* version, as well as *the Bell Jar* version, and G-d help us, the *Enemies: A Love Story* version. I personally favor the Lemony Snicket *Series of Unfortunate Events* version which comes in 13 scrolls, has pictures, was made into a movie, as well as a video-game (although the movie is stupid), and gives you a pretty good idea of what it's like to be any kind of decent person in a complicated, morally ambiguous world. In **The Grim Grotto**, Scroll 11, for example, a man with a hook for a hand observes that people are like a chef's salad generally and have

both good things and bad things all mixed up inside of them, but that they aren't generally all good or evil.

Now *that's* what I call Torah.

Maimonides, Mitzvah 23:
To honor those who teach and know Torah — Lev. 19:32

Manic Maven:

Of course you should honor the people who teach and learn Torah, in this extended understanding of the term, which I have just set forth in the preceding mitzvah. Honor means pay them if they are working for you, and write them a fan letter if they are famous, and go hear them read or do a public event, and buy their books, and ask INTELLIGENT questions during the Q and A. **Nota bene**: please *don't* use the Q and A portion as an excuse to talk about YOUR OWN sorry-ass attempt at a Torah project, because it's not ALL ABOUT YOU, so be respectful of these more accomplished and learned folks for once.

Maimonides, Mitzvah 24:
Not to inquire into idolatry — Lev. 19:4

Manic Maven:

It's never a good idea to ask a complete stranger: "what's that weird statue you're toting around?" or "why are you kneeling before that icon?" On the other hand, it's perfectly acceptable to allow visiting friends from out of town to stand respectfully in front of the revolving doors at the Bloomingdale's flagship store, because it *is* fabulous.

Maimonides, Mitzvah 25:
Not to follow the whims of your heart or what your eyes see —
<u>Num. 15:39</u>

Manic Maven:

In other words, do you really need that 4th pair of Uggs, and do you really want to have oral sex with your:

Student
Professor
Sister in law
Daughter in law
Massage Therapist
Dental Hygienist (because the dentist is too busy or isn't your type)
Attorney
Gardener
Barista
Rabbi
Neighbor's attractive Teenager
Librarian
Firefighter Captain
Plumber (who lives across the street, is 25, Irish and has several well-placed tattoos)
???????

If upon reflection, the answer to any of the above is an enthusiastic, heartfelt "yes!" then you probably still shouldn't do it. But--let's put it this way--I *understand*.

Glimmer and Blossom (Hans Arp, "Gluehen und Bluehen")

Hey man, got any roses for sale?
How about some stars?
What is a glimmering blossoming star going for these days?
We'd like to buy us some of that glimmer and blossom.
But how expensive is it?
Does it really cost as much as a lifetime? (seems pricey)

My heart blossoms says the heart.
Ashes and dust answers the emptiness.
My heaven glimmers says the heart.
Ashes and dust answers the emptiness.

Well, heck we'd still like to buy us those roses
we'd still like to buy us some stars
so
why don't we ask our buddy the Tightrope Walker
if glimmering and blossoming really costs a lifetime (both of ours? really?)

Honey, will you LOOK at our friend the Tightrope Walker--
She's a star of the first magnitude isn't she?
How gorgeous, how gorgeous she
glimmers and blossoms on that tightrope
how she balances--and--perfectly--
glistens and blooms

O Newcomer (Joachim Du Bellay, "nouveau venu qui cherches Rome à Rome")

You who just got off the plane at LAX--yeah YOU! -- you're seeking LA in LA
But you can't fucking find it can you? No. No one can.
LA's a weird town--there's no there there, and it's a kind of monument to itself:
a sprawling cemetery of dream factories at once here and not here.
You want the streets paved with stars? That's Hollywood. You're looking for the
beach? That's Santa Monica.
As for Los Angeles proper, there's a bit of it downtown by the train station,
downtown near
where John Fante lived.
They're trying to protect those old buildings now, but a lot got ripped out.
So--quick--go see the graffiti on the LA River channels before the city erases
It or floods it away.
Take a look at that river. It's just a trickle, right? But still, it flows.
Funny, how what struggles to remain is destroyed
while what's fluid, even though it's small--
persists.

I am who I am (Jacques Prévert, "je suis comme je suis")

I am who I am
I am just made like this.
I laugh when I want to laugh.
I love whoever loves *me*.
Is it my fault that it's not the same person
That I love each and every single time?
How is that your business?
What do you want from my life?
Why do you want to change me?

I'm made to please and *what's
so bad about that*?
My hands are like this.
My waist is like this.
My eyes are like this.
My breasts are like this.
I kiss like this.
I love like this.

I am who I am
How is that your business?
I please who I please.
What's it to you anyway?

Yes, it happened to me once
That I really loved someone once
and yes that someone really loved me--
like children we loved
simple simple. love love.
If you don't like it, ok.
If you don't want me, ok.
I please who I please
and I'm not going to change
anything.

Maria Stuart on Mars: An Impossible One Act Drama in Non-Verse (Friedrich Schiller, *Maria Stuart*)

Scene: Mars. Red dirt. Piles of Louis Vuitton luggage are carted on the stage by workpersons in drab. Cases in various stages of being unpacked. Slips, pearls robes, velvet, 3 boxes of Kleenex. In the center open hatbox: a diadem.

A CHORUS of MARTIAN WOMEN *surveys the arrival of the baggage with interest. Muttering and pointing in Martian.*

MARIA STUART: *takes off astronaut's helmet. MARTIAN WOMEN gaze upon her.*

Spotlight on MARIA.

MS: Martian women, I am undecided as to where to put my luggage and what to do, as I have landed here through an unexpected space-time break thanks to a machine made by Friedrich Schiller, then thrown into the future and then thrown back again, transporting me at the moment of my supposed execution to this spot.

MARTIAN WOMEN: we have heard of you.

MS: *unpacking suitcases. Tosses out gloves, pocketbooks, handkerchiefs.* What have you heard?

MARTIAN WOMEN: We heard that you were the villain.

MS: *unpacking: high-heeled boots, slippers, mules, sneakers, vans, flip flops, stops at the Birkenstocks.*

I am not the villain. I am the hero. The villain is—

Spaceship touches down. Steam, dry ice. Roaring of engines.

Elizabeth I, Regina, *gets out in a typical Elizabeth I dress with a typical Elizabeth I hairstyle, wearing a ww1 gas mask.*

MS: Behold!

Elizabeth R: Greetings Martians! Although I am but a woman I have the heart and stomach of k-- *sees Maria.*

MS: Not that same old speech.

MARTIAN WOMEN: We need to tell you something.

ER: How did you get here first?

MS: Schiller.

ER: Those fucking Germans.

MARTIAN WOMEN: *consternation and various comments are made.* She said the f-word. Who is Schiller? The friend of Goethe's. You mean the one who wrote Faust? Who's' Faust and so on.

MS: I claim Mars in the name of Scotland.

ER: I claim Mars in the name of England.

MARTIAN WOMEN: We don't know how to tell you this, but this planet has already has been claimed --

Sound of electric guitar...

MS and ER engage *in a fierce tug of war over a long velvet cloak that rips in two, sending them both clattering to the floor. As this happens they recite appropriate passages from the actual confrontation in the Schiller play OR different speeches from same.*

MS and ER together: BY WHOM?

Sound of familiar electric guitar riff.

Back up band descends on wires.

Lead Guitarist: Are y'all ready?

MARTIAN WOMEN *start wiggling and screaming:*
        YES WE ARE READY.

Guitarist: Here he is the one the only...

Large man descends in lamé jumpsuit.

Guitarist: ELVIS.

ELVIS descends holding a small statue of himself, as band plays "Blue Suede Shoes" riff.

ELVIS: don't step on my blue suede shoes. *Looks at the Vuitton cases.* Nice bags, y'all. *Looks at the queens appreciatively.* I mean the LUGGAGE, and not you fine lookin' ladies.

MS: How did you get here, Mr. Presley?

MARTIAN WOMEN: We brought him here by means of the statue. Leader shows a National Inquirer newspaper from the 90's, whose headlines read STATUE OF ELVIS FOUND ON MARS. The statue was dropped here, and we wanted this man as our king. We created a spaceship and brought the whole band.

MS: Typical.

ER: Typical. They always prefer a man.

MS: So, does that mean you and I can be friends? Sisters?

ER: No fucking way.

MARTIAN WOMEN: Elizabeth certainly has a dirty mouth.

ElVIS *does a double take of pleasure seeing the diadem in its Vuitton hat case. He takes the diadem and puts it on his head.*
    I am the king, and you both can be my queens.

MS: *Looks at Elizabeth, starts repacking.*
    I guess I'll go back to the chopping block. I thought this would be an improvement.

MARTIAN WOMEN *turn to Elizabeth*: We will accept you, as our queen.

EP to ER: And I will accept YOU as mine.

ER *considers but is clearly pleased to be thought more attractive than MS*:
    I like to be the boss.

EP: Ok, just as long as I can borrow your dress sometimes. Don't you have any other luggage?

ER: No.

EP *snaps his fingers as – garment racks get wheeled in from left and right.*

That's ok; you can borrow some of my stuff.

MS: I think I was not meant to survive. I represent some other possibility not fully understood. *She gets out her cell phone. She speaks into it.*

Freddy--come pick me up. We need to try something else.

A wormhole opens up, and FRIEDRICH SCHILLER appears, resplendent in late 18th century garb, and riding a motorcycle with sidecar. Schiller extends his hand.

MS grabs the nearest Vuitton suitcase, waves goodbye and goes.

THE END

that time (William Shakespeare, "That time of year thou mayest in me behold")

that time I almost died—in the winter when there was no rain
and it was cold, unseasonably, that time at the Philarmonic—
That time I fainted as the orchestra played and the light was orange
fading in the west of my vision as I went under my eyes still open.
Like a preview of Death—I passed out and came back and saw the EXIT sign—
and I heard your voice.
And what I hope is this:
Then when I really go, your voice will take me there.

red (Paul Verlaine, "Green")

here are red velvet cupcakes, raspberries, red wine, and chocolate
on a tray near the bed--and voilà--my nakedness that
stirs and rustles only for you
mold it with your two hands
and may those hands be gentle--or not.

I arrive barely conscious still from desert sleep
the dry morning wind already heating up the quilts:
awaken me, with feet, torso, lips--
Let the dreams fade out around your immediate warmth.

I roll my head on your younger-than-me belly
still ringing with the images I no longer remember;
I want to close my eyes, re-capture them--but no
you say. this is not any longer a time to sleep.

mummy (Sylvia Plath, "Dadd*y*")

Mummy was a Nazi--
we don't like to say it
because it's an *über*-inconvenient truth
ach du--and especially not very pleasant

in a mother. she had small jew shoes
that never fit me, and when she was
thin I couldn't fit into her little Russian dresses either

but she did like Wagner--which let's face it
is suspicious
but what was worse, *liebe freunde*
really *mehr* worse
is how she put herself in the oven
made of herself a holocaust--
yes I know that's in bad taste
but what do you do with a *mutter*
who pulled that SS shit on *herself,*
on her body, and left me to be in
charge of the *sonderkommando*
going through the wreckage
of her exiled life
searching through the sewn-in-the-skirt-hems gems
for mine?

Online Summary of the <u>Book of the City of Ladies</u> (Christine de Pizan, *Livre de la Cité des Dames*)

CDAM. 1211d.01   Description: Here commences the table of rubrics of the medieval artifact *the book of the city of ladies* which has 1,2,3, parts and the first part starts with a wall that surrounds us with safety and cocktails.

item 0: here begin the chapters and they are **cool.**

item 1: Christine says ḣí everyƀoðy and guess wḣat? tḣese 3 faðies appeareð to me wḣen I got ðepresseð watcḣing **Busty Cops** anð **Girfs Gone Wifð** anð notḣing but tḣe objectification of women anð girfs on TV anð ḣatreð of tḣe feminine in alf its guises (but a kinð of screweð up fascination too) on tḣe internet anð it just bummeð me out, so I felf asfeep ḣað fike a VISIO2t.

[translatrix's note: what follows is an allegory--which means it's symbolic in a kind of direct relationship sort of way, so here we go!]

item 2: Christine says that lady #1 who was REASON told her that she was her own property, aka she belonged to herself and so she had been chosen because she was nice and also needed the money to build the city of ladies and Christine of course said

 a) 2twesome and then

b) Merci!

item 3 says more about how **Lady Reason** told her how to make the walls and drain the swamps and do all the junk you have to do to get a city in order, yo.

item 4: Christine reports how the second lady told her name and her name was a great name--it was RIGHTS, and that Christine needed to serve Lady Rights and make the RIGHTS of all women known.

item 5: the third lady said her name was **JUSTICE** (which is straightforward symbolism but it's great because we CERTAINLY NEED JUSTICE STILL IN THE 21ST CENTURY [translatrix's note])and after that there are a lot more items

items 6-36-- there's disputation and defense because after all this is the Middle Ages so they have to do all that very formal, recitation of argument and then rebuttal and I guess it's from the Greeks or the Romans, and that goes on for quite a while, but at the end they say yeah let's build, and Christine

builds the allegorical city which is a defense of femininity and she writes about how great it is in another

book and **there are all kinds of illuminated**

manuscripts showing Christine with her

BOOK, saying that women are cool and good, and everybody's a lady and stuff like that. If it were written now ladies would include everybody who indentifies as a lady whether you have a vagina or a penis or both or *nothing* or something DIFFERENT and Christine would say that if you say you are a lady and identify as a lady, then you *are* a lady and the reason she's using the word lady is to try to let the king and the court know that women are important, although you're right - it is a class thing, but still *city of ladies* sounds nice so I'm going to stay with that translation [yes, this is the translatrix talking again, but now I'm jazzed about this whole project so what the hell, I'm here very openly translating and explaining this chef d'oeuvre instead of pretending I'm an invisible God-writerperson].

In other words:

a. *The Book of the City of Ladies* is pre-wave feminism, which should flow into the 3rd and 4th waves and beyond to **beyond** the place where everything is *gendered.*

b. There are other cities than Troy and Los Angeles and Moscow, and Beijing, and Dubai and Mumbai and Lima and Austin and Oslo and Toronto, and Cairo and Bamako since we're rhyming right here. There are other cities and we can imagine them and if we can imagine them, we can make them real. And even if we can't make them real right away, we can start by imagining, and so we still need we really need our visions.

So let them come. Let's start dreaming.

click on the following links for more information:

contact Christine de Pizan

About Christine and her books

Donate/give/help

Build your own city (what are you waiting for?)

What is the what (author unknown, *Book Of Jonah* עשר תרי])

Jonah said to God what is the what?
And God said you got to go talk to those people
Over there, and Jonah said sure and promptly
Took a one-way cruise to nowhere, because THOSE people,
They were no good mothers and then a lady (who probably was a **real** mother)
on the boat said,
You're *messhuge*. If God says you got to do something
Then You BETTER do it. Ok, old lady, said Jonah putting
On the sunblock in his deck chair, but then the monster
Came--like in one of those old movies--and he got swallowed
Up and it was disgusting inside that animal, and so Jonah
Climbed out and got on the metrolink
And went to that crap suburb where the really jerk people live
And he said what is the what, and they said what?
and he said
Listen.

Psalm 23 for the 21st Century (*Psalms* [מִילְהָת])

the lord is my real estate agent I shall not want for
open houses. she maketh me to re do the paint job
she leadeth me through the process of redecorating
for the sake off the first impressions
yea though there is a serious mold issue growing
underneath the house, I fear not for she has the
subcontractors clearing out the mess. her organizer
named Ian and her assistant named Sharon they
comfort me with coffees and places to put my pocket books.
My realtor has set the table in the presence of all the potential buyers
and has set the price *high*. my savings account runneth over
with unexpected dividends and I shall dwell in my new house
in the Palisades for a good long time, or at least until
I move into an even better house up north. amen

On the bridge of Los Angles (anonymous, "Sur le Pont D'Avignon")

on the bridge
where's the bridge?
there's no bridge here--
let's dance anyway

here in LA.

if you identify as male--you bow like *this*
if you identify as female--you curtsey like *this*
if you identify as neither --you twirl like *this*

on the bridge
though there *is* no bridge
we're going to dance anyway

we dig dancing
in LA

if you are a leftist--you cavort like *this*
if you are an anarchist--you pirouette like *this*
if you are both --you jump for joy like *this*

we'll make pretend bridges
though we have no bridges
with our selves we'll make bridges
over non-existent waterways--
here in LA.
See--we're going to dance *anyway*
so let's take hands
make a circle right now.

Overpriced shoes (Elinor Wylie, "Velvet Shoes")

Let us walk in overpriced shoes on the polished floors
of South Coast Plaza before the crowds come, circa 9 am;
with big steps because I'm exercising with the stroller,
trying to burn some calories,
before I meet the only friend I have in Orange County
for lunch.

I shall visit the ESPRIT store (those clothes that mesh punk with country club)
and you are a baby so you are sleeping in a baby ESPRIT outfit
that is covered with milk, because you threw up a little.
It hardens and is just now drying
on your chest like a crust.

We shall walk along the corridors
windless because they haven't turned on the air–conditioning,
We shall step on the clean floors, so white because they're
bleached,
and a lady in a smock is laying the bleach right down the way
from us and a man in orange is operating the buffer.

We shall walk in overpriced shoes be they Addidas or Ecco or
even Arche wherever we go, but isn't it nice to
feel the silence of pre–shopping, your own little feet clad
in slippers from Germany?
the buzzing of the floor polisher and the hissing of the sliding open
store doors
as we traipse the halls with our money.

The O'Henriad (Homer, *The Iliad* ['Oμηρος, Ἰλιάς])

Once upon a time, a writer named O. Henry published a story that everyone but my mother loved. It was called "The Gift of the Magi," and it was about a couple who loved each other so much—well you know the drill. Mr. O. Henry became such a household name that Swanky Snacks confectioners approached him about making a candy bar named after him.

"That sounds positively scrumptious," said Mr. O. Henry, who was working hard on his new story about kidnappers who abduct a small boy so obnoxious that they pay the parents to take him back.

The O. Henry bar was a big hit.

But this candy bar invention was to have drastic repercussions.

* * *

"Goddamn it," roared Ernest Hemingway at breakfast in Key West. "Shirley, did you read about this fucking O. Henry bar?" The famous author threw the *Wall Street Journal* on top of the French toast, sopping it in maple syrup, while the current Mrs. Hemingway cleaned up the wine bottles and the cigar butts and the broken glassware from another one of the grand old man of American Literature's notorious parties.

"That jerk O. Henry has a candy bar named after him and I don't," Hemingway hollered again for effect.

"Yes, dear," said Mrs. Hemingway. She looked up at him from the dustpan, summoning her most winning smile. "I'm sure it tastes positively dreadful!" she said.

But Hemingway would not be appeased.

"Get on the horn, Shirley, and talk to the other authors, and see how they are taking the news," said Hemingway, spitting out bits of French toast.

"Right away, dear," said Mrs. Hemingway. She went to the desk and got out her tidy, little red leather address book with the name FAMOUS AUTHORS on it and started phoning like mad.

First, she phoned France.

"Mrs. Camus?" said Mrs. Hemingway. "Ernest is in a terrible state about this candy bar situation."

"Oui, je sais," said Mrs. Camus as she ironed her famous husband's white shirts. "Albert is *absolument furieux*. He demands a nonexistential, absurdist confection of his own *tout de suite*, and the man from Godiva is coming over from Brussels today to draw up the agreement."

"Bon," said Mrs. Hemingway. She hesitated. "Or should I say *bonbon!"* The two women giggled nervously and hung up because this was an overseas call and quite expensive.

Camus—check.

Mrs. Hemingway proceeded down the list of famous authors:

Eco. *"Si, certo—gia fato,"* said Mrs. Eco when Mrs. Hemingway called. That very day, Mrs. Eco reported, Umberto struck a deal with the Perugina people to make small chocolates—soon to be known as the famous *Baci*—that would please the maestro.

Eco—check.

Grass. The housekeeper conveyed that Herr Grass was away at a recovering Nazi collaborators convention, but when he came back, he was sure to kick up a rumpus. Fearing the uproar, Frau Grass had already left for Switzerland on the afternoon train to talk to the Suchard people about a grass-green chocolate bar to reveal the ecological sympathies of the author.

Grass—check.

Nabokov—Stoli Brand, chocolate-flavored vodka. Check.

The Europeans seem to have the matter well in hand, thought Mrs. Hemingway with satisfaction. *Let's see what's happening in Latin America.*

Mrs. Hemingway phoned Sally Neruda, whom she'd known at Wellesley. Sally told her—over a very broken connection—that indeed civil war had broken out in all the countries over this chocolate author insult, which was regarded as yet another imperialist, typically North American maneuver.

Mrs. Betsy Bolaño confirmed that the Latin-American writers were—to the man— predictably enraged. Notable exceptions Clarice Lispector and Elena Poniatowska immediately organized the homeless of Mexico City into a people's chocolate-making collective. They began fabricating their own chocolates, which they sent to the chocolate-loving proletariat in poor countries around the world. Nadine Gordimer flew over from Cape Town to help with the shipments.

Isabel Allende could not be reached for comment, but it was apparently *she* who called Salman Rushdie about these latest developments.

And that's when the nougat really hit the fan.

in only (ee cummings "in just spring")

in only summer
when larry and stephanie
are barreling down Queen Anne for
blueberries and froyo
and it's humid--
and the tall paraplegic
war vet wishes
us
a
good evening

and georgy and billy
come with custom
backpacks to the church
where the AA sign hangs
discretely-- two blue
letters--and the tall paraplegic
war vet sits with a sign that says
WOUNDED IN THIS WAR

and the girl with the pixy cut
and the guy who wants to be manager
walk out of the old hotel saying
I wish I could quit and I hate it I hate it
as the gaunt paraplegic vet sits watching
the traffic lights go off and on, and the buses
move along mercer and he holds
his sign
and wishes us peace.

Acknowledgements

"Ars Judaica" originally appeared in *Sex with Buildings*, Dancing Girl Press, 2012.

"Boxes and Bags" originally appeared in *CRATE*, 2006.

"Eve" originally appeared in *Mosaic*, 1999.

"Madness in the Method" originally appeared in *CRATE*, 2009.

"Maria Stuart on Mars" originally appeared in *Sex with Buildings*, Dancing Girl Press, 2012.

"The O'Henriad" originally appeared in *Pearl*, 2010.

"Old Chocolate," originally appeared in *Mosaic*, 1999.

"Sestina (fake) for Chrysler, my father, and me" originally appeared in *Soundings*, 2010.

"Sister Sabbath" originally appeared in *Mosaic*, 2000.

"Torah Bones" originally appeared in *Bridges*, 2000.

"Woman to Woman" originally appeared in *Sex with Buildings*, Dancing Girl Press, 2012.

The author wishes to thank the following people, institutions and entities –living, dead, fictional, and real

Anyone kind whom I may have forgotten

Dancing Girl Press

Dave Baraff

Kerry Bar-Cohen

Jeffrey Batchelor

Judy Behrendt

Larry Behrendt

Lillian Behrendt

Belgian Village Camp

Erith Jaffe Berg

Gordon Berger

Beyond Baroque

Anne Boochever

Delphine Boswell

Kristy Bowen

Ann Brantingham

Archie Brantingham

John Brantingham

Tim Buckley

Cheddar Cheese

Chevalier Books

Children of Paradise

Sheryl Clough

Jean Cocteau

Jo Scott Coe

Justin Scott Coe

ee cummings

Eulene

Ana Maria Fagundo

The Fall

Leone Fogle

French

Tess Gallagher

German

Idee German

Robert Gross

Andrea Grossman

Hair Club for Poets

Barbé Hammer

Leonard Hammer

Marie Hartung

Donna Hilbert

Inlandia Institute

Judy Kronenfeld

Ashia Lane

Leuchtturm 1917

Los Angeles Red Line

Los Angeles Union Station

Manhattan

Jeffrey McDaniel

milk chocolate

the Mission Inn

Robert Murphy

Hilary Henry Neff

Elizabeth Newstat

Northwest Institute of
Literary Arts

Vivian Nyitray

Pain Quotidien

Cati Porter

Physicists

Rabbis for Human Rights

Rashi

Riverside Rapid Transit

Bruce Holland Rogers

Gwen Samelson

San Gabriel Valley Literary
Festival

Sandra Sarr

Roy Anthony Shabla

Elena Secota and the Rapp
Saloon

Theda Shapiro

soy lattes

Erika Suderburg

Soundings Literary Review

Students

William Van Voris

Whole Foods Market

Wine makers of North
America, France, South
America. and the world

Carolyne Wright

Jill Berkson Zimmerman

About the Author

Descended from Norwegian plumbers on one side, and bohemian Russian aristocrats on the other, Stephanie Barbé Hammer wrote her first poem at 6 and has never stopped loving poems. She has published short fiction and poetry in Mosaic, The Bellevue Literary Review, Pearl, NYCBigCityLit, Rhapsoidia, CRATE, and the Hayden's Ferry Review among other places. She has been nominated for a Pushcart Prize 4 times – most recently, in 2013, for her non-fiction work on converting to Judaism and her relationship with French. Her prose poem chapbook, Sex with Buildings, was published with Dancing Girl Press in May 2012. She is the recent recipient of an MFA from the Northwest Institute of Literary Arts and she is currently working on a series of novels about a secret branch of Anabaptists who use puppets for their rituals. A former New Yorker, Stephanie divides her time between Los Angeles, California and Coupevillle, Washington. She lives with her husband, Larry Behrendt, at least 2 unfinished knitting projects, and a bunch of cookbooks whose covers she has never cracked.

CPSIA information can be obtained
at www.ICGtesting.com
Printed in the USA
FSHW02n1304200918
52424FS